Ru

D1448387

ISLAND

ISLAND

Collected Poems

KENNETH STEVEN

SAINT ANDREW PRESS
Edinburgh

First published in 2009 by
SAINT ANDREW PRESS
121 George Street
Edinburgh EH2 4YN

Copyright © Kenneth Steven, 2009

ISBN 978 0 7152 0909 7

All rights reserved. No part of this publication may be reproduced or transmitted in any form or by any means, electronic or mechanical, including photocopy, recording, or information storage and retrieval system, without permission in writing from the publisher. This book is sold subject to the condition that it shall not, by way of trade or otherwise, be lent, resold, hired out or otherwise circulated without the publisher's prior consent.

The right of Kenneth Steven to be identified as author of this work has been asserted in accordance with the Copyright, Designs and Patents Act 1988.

British Library Cataloguing in Publication Data
A catalogue record for this book is available from the British Library.

It is the publisher's policy to only use papers that are natural and recyclable and that have been manufactured from timber grown in renewable, properly managed forests. All of the manufacturing processes of the papers are expected to conform to the environmental regulations of the country of origin.

Typeset in Zapf Book by Waverley Typesetters, Fakenham
Printed and bound in the United Kingdom by MPG Books Ltd, Bodmin

CONTENTS

Many of these poems have appeared in literary magazines in the UK, the United States, Canada and Australia. Some have been included in anthologies; a good number have been translated and published in Scots Gaelic, German, Norwegian and Icelandic. Many have been broadcast on BBC Radio 3 and 4, and on BBC Radio Scotland.

In the Beginning

There was nothing but everything

A robin opened the jewellery of his throat

The moon grew and ballooned the skies

A horse ran through a starlit field

Somewhere a stream sang its own song

Primroses broke from the dark to open their eyes

And someone came barefoot into warm sunlight

▦ FIRE

Through the blurred lens of memory
I see a man
Cutting peats on the bare moon of a moorland.

All the stones that build his world are Gaelic:
Fishing, mending, stories, singing, prayers –
London's out of touch, a blurred voice on the radio.

All day his back bends and the blade shapes
Drenched, dark wedges of peat
That are stacked to dry in the summer wind.

Inside each slab the ferns of Culloden, of clearance,
Of the battle to evict starvation –
Imprints of history like fossils.

This is the peat that lights the memory,
That fires the struggle,
That keeps the heart burning.

IONA FERRY

It's the smell I remember –
The dizziness of diesel, tarry rope, wood sheened
   like toffee.
The sea was waving in the wind, a dancing –
I wanted it to be rough and yet I didn't.
My mother and I snugged under the awning,
To a dark rocking. We were as low as the waves,
All of us packed in tight like bales of wool.

The engine roared alive, its tremor
Juddered through the wood and thrilled me, beat
   my heart.
The shore began fading behind the white curl of our
   hum.
Fourteen days lay barefoot on the island –
Still asleep, their eyes all shut.
And yet I knew them all already,
Felt them in my pocket like polished stones –
Their orchids, their hurt-white sand, their larksong.

◈ THE STARS

From the age of five my sight was smudged as a
    mole's;
I wore tortoiseshell-rimmed glasses that were never
    quite clean
And the stars looked white and indistinct
Vague pearls in a distant heaven.
On my fifteenth birthday my parents gave me
    lenses –
Little cupped things that drifted into sight across my
    irises.
Driving home with them that night I suddenly caught
    sight of something,
Got out by the edge of the field and looked,
Amazed and disbelieving as if Christ himself had
    healed my eyes,
For the stars were crackling and sparking
Like new-cut diamonds on the velvet of a jeweller's
    window,
So near and clear I could have stretched and held
    them,
Carried them home in my own pocket.
That was the gift my parents gave me on my
    birthday –
The stars.

⌖ SATURDAYS

We used to go there for eggs –
A farm track with that green vein
Sprouting the middle rut. The farm crouched
Like some aggressive wildcat on the ground
Whose yellow eyes were windows. The whole yard
    strutted
And bagpiped with chickens. I always feared the
    dogs –
Two streamlined waterfalls of black and white,
Tongues like hot bacon, their barks
Gunning my heart with fear. But the farmer's wife
Brought us inside to the kitchen's hum,
The scent of mown hay green in the room.
We talked about foxes and new roads and prices,
My lips burned on hot tea. The eggs were still warm,
Dunged and tickled with straw.
We squeaked them in sixes into boxes,
Went out across the yard as a blue sky
Switched with swallows, waved to her wide smile
On the long bounce home.

☒ ANNA

The river, slack in August heat,
Silted grey-blue through the trees.
The sun was a hammer beating brass,
Dizzying our heads.

Our backs stooped to strawberries –
Nipping the stalks, tumbling them into punnets –
As the farmer bellowed along the rows,
Bulling us loud to work.

But Anna was gold like wheat, shining from long
    summer,
Her hair ringed around her shoulders;
She laughed, told stories,
Pushed the other boys so my heart drummed.

At noon we scuffed the track, darkened the cool of
    the barn,
Dropped down in the hay to eat. I sat behind her,
A hundred questions in my head like circling
    wasps –
Yet not one ever reached my lips.

I dreamed of going barefoot to the river,
Plashing the low water, watching still
For flicks of fish that daggered through the pools,
And touching hands and swimming till the dark.

Now she's just a wild scent in my head –
A flower pressed, an imprint left on years
Gone long ago. Only when I bend each August for the
    strawberries
I touch a place called Anna in my mind.

⬙ THE BIRTH OF THE FOAL

My eyes still fought with sleep. Out over the fields
Mist lay in grey folds, from vague somewheres
Curlews rose up with thin trails of crying. Our
    lanterns
Rocked in soft globes of yellow, our feet
Slushed through the early morning thickness of the
    grass.

She lay on her side, exhausted by her long night;
The hot smell of flanks and head and breath
Ghosted from her spread length.
Sunlight cracked from the broken yolk of the skies,
Ruptured the hills, spangled our eyes and blinded
    us,
Flooded the pale glows of our lanterns.

There he lay in a pool of his own wetness:
Four long spindles scrabbling, the bigness of his
    head, a bag of a body –
All struggling to find one another, to join up, to glue
Into the single flow of a birthright. He fought
For the first air of his life, noised like a child.

His mother, still raw and torn from the scar of his
    birth,
Turned, and her eyes held him,
The great harsh softness of her tongue stilled his
    struggle.

We knelt in the wet grass, dumbed
By a miracle, by something bigger than the sun.

◈ DAFFODILS

They flurry over the first raw green of the hills,
Trumpet the Easter fields;
Bright flags with their orange yolks
Bending under the flaying cruelty of April winds.

As if to prove that Calvin got it wrong,
That dark-lipped Luther in the cold austerity of
  history
Threw away the warm laughter of love
For the bare bones of theology.

◈ ABERNETHY

Just within sight of a blue wing of the Tay,
Where it silts and silvers out to sea –
A place made of pantiles, all lime and yellow
In the middle of July. We went inside
To the sudden, cool hold of the shop,
Unchanged, perhaps, since the days of soldiers,
The rationing years, the echoes of bombs on
     Glasgow.
The old woman's face shone like an onion,
Her knife-cuts of eyes glimmered and smiled –
This ice cream is the last in the world, she said –
And somehow I believed her, watching the silky
     waves
Flow from the metal, the papers she carefully curled
To wrap them inside. I wondered if she knew
We had changed, if she'd seen the prices
Outside, in the fast world
That was turning to machines.

▣ CLONMACNOISE

Wrapped in the wool of winter
The fields breathed with frost

Even the Shannon confused
Searching in ribbons through the fields

The sun straining to see
Like a single frozen eye

We came to Clonmacnoise
Fifteen hundred years too late

Crows in the ivied silence of round towers
Gravestones bent as though in penitence

Chapels fallen in upon themselves
Like broken faith

And yet I could imagine
In the once upon a time of Ireland

Men awakening to break the wells
To bring in steamings of white water

Keeping the turf fire's glow
Storm after December storm

Here where they had caught God's light
(So fragile, yet alive for ever)

To bear it bright
Out into the dark places of the earth

THE ILLUMINATED MANUSCRIPT

They brought me here from Ireland, still a boy
To begin their book.

I remember the day I left –
Soft bread, a silvering of geese, the sound of my
    mother.

Now I slip the stone of these steps every day
Long before dawn, breathe the dark

And hear the whelming of the winds about this
    fastness
Before my one candle like a petal of gorse

Flutters the shadows in ghosts over the cold walls.
Out of the thin window I watch the sea all winter

Heave and drag like a dying man,
The skies blackened and bruised.

Some days there is nothing in the pen except
My own emptiness; I hold it hoping

Until the stars blow out from the attic of the skies
And a ledge of moon lifts across the hills.

Just sometimes something breaks inside
Like the brittle lid of a casket

And pours out light onto the waiting page.

▣ Mushrooms

The night before a great moon full of honey
Had flowed up behind the hills and poured across
   the fields.

The leaves were rusting, the wheat whispered
Dry and gold in the wind's hands.

Andrew and I went to Foss. We drove over the hills
That were blustery with huge gusts of sunlight.

We stopped and walked to the loch, left two trails
Through the grass, came on the mushrooms by
   accident,

A village of strewn white hats
The folds of their gills underneath as soft as skin.

We almost did not want to take them, as if
It would be theft – wronging the hills, the trees, the
   grass.

But in the end we did, we picked them with
   reverence:
And they broke like bread between our hands, we
   carried them home,

Pieces of field, smelling of earth and autumn;
A thanksgiving, a blessing.

MEETING

Today I met a journeyman thatcher.
He had not been born with that life in his blood;
One day he just dug up his roots and left,
Never looked back.

He said that sometimes as he swept the thatch
Up onto a roof and heard the shingle of the trees,
The fields' chase, he was blown
Out of the mad motorway of this age

To a place that you never could buy,
A place that is on no map.
He had heard it and touched it in roofs,
In thatch, just once or twice, for a moment.

In him now the back lanes, the side roads
Of a timeless time, a land where hay ricks
Still jolt and topple. I sensed the sunlight in him
Warm as a whole summer.

THE ARTISTS

Her father sold canvases in Paris
In the black and white days before war
Drowned the young men of Europe
In the mud of their own blood.
He sold canvases to the artists
Who lived down dark nowheres
In bare attics and huddled cellars.
He watched them go from the shop, shaking his head
At the yellow stains of their fingers
The old smell of their clothes.
He knew the hard bargain of money
They failed to comprehend.

But one night in July
He saw them leave for the country
His canvases in their bags,
And the gourd of the moon poured over them,
Poured over them and their laughter.
He stood there, alone and dark,
As they went searching the sound of the wheat,
The colour of the air,
The scent of the starlight.

THE KINGFISHER

One early May we went there, on foot,
Through the ghostly cobwebs of the morning,
Hearing the curlews rising in hauntings across the
    fields.
The land was muddy, a guttural rushing of syllables
After long spring rain, so our boots were sucked and
    glutted
By a swilling of mire. We struggled through screens
    of trees,
Nets of rain meshing our faces, till we broke out
By that little trickle of stream –
Nothing more than a slither of thick water
Rippling away in different shades of inks.

Then, from nowhere, that blue bolt came
Bright as a dragonfly, a bit of summer sky,
Low as some skiffed stone, threading the reeds
To catch a branch, to lock
Into the sapphire thrill of kingfisher.
We stood amazed, gazing, ages,
Unable to believe the piece of luck we'd stumbled on.
We have kept that blue ever since
Somewhere in the winter attics of our world –
A priceless place, a whole kingdom.

A Day In April

Twelve o'clock. She stands in the back porch,
Strands of gold hair tangling her face.
She calls his name; her voice is blown away.
He looks up nonetheless, as though he's heard
Somewhere deep inside. Light scours the hills,
Gullies of wind sweep back the shadow.
Fleet's heard her, flows down the field
In a bouncing waterfall of black and white.
She smiles. A lamb pities the air
With a cry as thin as milk. She turns inside.

He thuds the mud from his boots.
Has the mail come? Delivery from Hulberts?
The clock flickers softly in the hall;
Up in the landing window the blue of April
A rippling flag of sky –
This land is in his hands
As surely as it ran his father's.
At the table she rumbles the potatoes from the pan,
Looks at him with soft eyes. I've good news, she
    murmurs.

THE HORSEMAN'S WORD

He did not know French or the history of art.
He did not know the declensions of verbs.
He did not know when Sir Christopher Wren
Built the dome of St Paul's Cathedral.

He knew the names of the songbirds,
He knew where the geese came to rest in autumn,
And he knew the one word
That could bridle a wild horse;
The word that had passed like a pearl
From mouth to mouth, son after son,
That secret whisper old as the fields themselves.

When his father lay
Washed up on the last tide of his life,
He gave his word
To the young, bright, blue well of a boy,
Who caught it and kept it,
Let it flow into the strong blood of his growing.

And later, when a whole galloping of horses
Had softened under his voice,
They envied him black
On the farms where they had books and learning
and stables;
They stared at him dumb, bewildered,

As he broke their stallions from wild thrashings of
    river
To beautiful waterfalls, creatures that poured
Into one word's gallop, that stilled
At the weight of a single hand.

He kept his word, his pearl,
Deep in the dark of his head –
A whole inheritance.

⬙ SHOES

The shoemaker stitched and sewed
In the dark scent of his own world. Once a year
I went in there, to the black adverts for boots and
    polish
Rusty over the walls of his shop. I blinked

Like something that had tumbled down a hole
Into the heart of the earth. Even the air was tanned,
The chestnut of shoes burnished and perfect from
    hands
That had poured in the pure oils of their love,

Their labour. He wiped those huge hands on his
    apron,
Stood as I smoothed my feet into the mended shoes,
Looking, his eyes like a calf's, brown,
In an air that was brown, a brown cave.

The scent of leather hung in the air,
In my shoes that were good as new,
That fitted my feet like hooves –
They shone so I saw my own smile.

I went out into the blue breeze of the springtime,
Watching my step, all the way home. Still,
School scuffed them and skinned them,
Reduced them at last to a shadow of all they had
    been.

THE WIND AND THE MOON

The wind woke me, the loud howl of it
Boomed round the house and I felt at sea;
I fastened my eyes and was out in a ship,
Ten miles of Atlantic. I went to the window,
Watched the whole round of the moon
Ploughing through clouds, a coin
Of silver and gold.

All night I was blown between dreams,
Never slept deep, was thinking
Of the trees crashing and rising with wind,
Of the chestnut rain that would fall
By the morning.

At dawn I woke up, went out
Into the bright blue whirl of the wind,
Rode the wild horse of it upwards
Into the wood and beyond,
To the hill with the chestnut trees,
The leaves dancing at my feet
Russet and gold.

I ran and ran till my chest
Hurt with my heart. Under the hands of the
   chestnuts

That waved and swung in the air,
Saddles of leather, polished and shining,
Broken from the beds of their shells –
A whole hoard.

I went home in a gust of light
My pockets and hands
Knobbled with conkers.

◈ THE SLIDE

We longed for the sharp crinkle of December stars,
That ghostly mist like cobwebs in the grass,
Ten degrees below zero.

After the snow came petalling from the skies,
Settled into a deep quilt, the frost
Diamonded the top, making a thick crust.

On the long descent of the lawn
We made our slide, planed the ground
Hour after hour till it smiled with ice.

At night we teetered out with buckets,
Rushed the buckets down the slide's length
In one black stain.

Next day the slide was lethal,
A curling glacier that shot us downhill
In a single hiss.

Even after the thaw greened our world again
The slide remained written in the grass
As long as our stories.

FREEDOM

After night, Edinburgh is spiced with frost.
The morning's blue, so pale it's almost white,
The oval of the moon above
Frail as the face of an old woman.

And in among the pearl-carved pillars and the
    plinths
Of Princes Street, the homeless sleep;
Underneath the doorways and the stairs they curl
Like hedgehogs.

As the wind picks up they shift and dig
A little deeper in their blankets, and some wake up
And blink and stare as I pass by.

As if their voices too have turned to ice,
As if they have forgotten where they are;
They do not even ask for money, only stare
Away into the April air.

And as I go I wonder,
If Scotland's freedom means a jot to them,
On this cold morning as they feel the empty gnaw
Of hunger, and the wind biting at their fingers and
    their faces
Like a dog.

STILL

beside the little chefs and the burger kings
the constant thrumming of engines in the lanes
that burn north and south to housing estates
that look the same in merseyside and melbourne

off the motorways and the dual carriageways
take a first left and then a right, drive on
down the bump and turning of a track you never
    knew
then thud the car door shut and stand and listen

the thin gracenotes of a lark twirling in a may sky
above the open saltmarsh and the early morning
    light
the sea's white kettledrums beyond, the burnished
    sun
goldening a whole deep field of buttercups and grass

THE STATE OF SCOTLAND

See this land through a broken window,
All huddled in mist, rocked by storm,
The whole long drudge of winter.

Half its people want to leave;
The other half who want to stay
Don't choose, they have no choice.

Our history is written in the hills. We are filled
With pride for what we think we did
And guilt for what we didn't do.

We drift into cities since we cannot stand
The sound of our own thoughts. We spend our lives
Being loud, and trying to forget.

Do we want freedom or just the chance
To mourn not having it? We are willing to fight
For all that we don't want.

❖ JOURNEY

One night the train took me no further than Stirling;
It was spring, a shiver of snow still lingering the hills.

I dug my way into the back of a taxi –
Tired, not wanting to talk the last miles home.

But the driver did. I had to lean forwards
To catch the rough edges of his words:

He'd been a miner
In the oldest pit in Scotland.

He missed it, he said, the cut and thrust of words
Down there in the dark –

The way men shaped their shout and banter
Deep in the shafts that gleamed and shone;

He missed it, he said –
One day the pit would open up again and he'd go
    back.

The air in the taxi filled
With his black-blue warmth of words.

And I realised he went back there every day
Still, to keep the place alive

Taking his passengers with him on the journey.
Outside the night went past as black as coal.

THE WOUND IN THE EARTH

All day under the circling
The golden hugeness of the sun
Beat by beat the maddening, terrible day
The terrible madness, until, suddenly, at last
The sky went ugly with bruises, a thunder stuttered
In the red hills and the rain came hard as grapes
Heavy, hissing, huge, and lightning gouged the dust.
His face, she saw his face, her son
The son she'd brought into a stable
Shining with bright rain and blood in rivers
And how his head slipped forwards, finished
His shoulders torn like wings, like angel wings
Broken now for ever by the weight
Of this last loss of God.
But even then they waited, the soldiers and the
    priests
Watching him with gaping mouths as if they still
    expected
He might speak or heal or teach.
They watched the rain shine his shoulders and his
    broken head
Hour after hour after hour
As if they feared him still.

COLUMBA

A film lies across the water meadows
like a muslin shawl. Birds lament
among rushes, their low voices trailing
like beads of glass. The sun has not been born yet,
remains under woods and hills.
Columba goes down, his ankles buried by soft water,
by green fronds, slippery, making no more sound
than a deer. The swans drift over the water,
so white they hurt the eyes. He stops,
forgetting everything as he watches the stoop and
    silver
of their grace, the sudden rippling of their backs
cast by wind, the furling of the huge wings
like shards of ice. They too are prayers,
personified, awakenings of God
in the morning water land.
He goes on, to the strange stone head
carved and lying dormant in the grass;
those wide eyes that never blinked,
the ringlets of stone hair curling
about the enigma of a half-buried face.
He comes here, even though the smiths who cut this
have known only gods of wood and loam,
have chanted under the wheels of stars,
made strange offerings of wheat and fire and gold.
Here at the water meadow's end he finds the Christ
ripe in his heart, his lips brim with words
that soar like larks into the sky,

almost as if some spring of light and joy
wells from the ground beneath.
He kneels in the wet softness of the earth
and smells the springtime yellow in his veins –
becomes the place he prays in.

The Bright Moment

All day the rain out of the west,
The telegraph wires looping through the mist,
Lambs lying wet in the edges of ditches,
Shivering, their mothers beside them like old stone.

We walked into the wind,
Fought our way to the loch
That fluttered and flamed, gusted greys and blacks –
And there on the water, together, two swans
Rising at our coming, flagging the wind,
Held together by the wind, those big buffetings –
Head and neck, head and neck, coupled
In the grey rambling of the sky.

And in that moment
I thought that nothing we had done or ever will
Could compare with this, this mastery of the sky, this
    storm dance –
And all I wanted always was to watch them.

CLARSACH

They had scarcely noticed her before.
A slip of a thing no more than sixteen,
A glitter of eyes and auburn hair –
It was November and they wanted nothing
But the peat fire and a whiskied head.
That first night she played the heads turned,
Fell away from their loose talk;
One by one they heard a rippling
Like the shudder of breeze over the black loch,
Like the unfurling of swans.
It was her hands –
The grace and flow of the fingers
Playing with the taut stems of the strings.
They saw their own hands then,
Lumped and ruddy, knuckled with fights.
She played them quiet. Like a long wave
She washed them ashore to the island
Where she wanted them, beached them
Dry and wondering, dog-eyed,
In the long echo that was left behind.

1914

It was a Saturday in October
And I had gone out in the sharp pain of bare feet
To the fields all starred with frost,
My mother's bucket thumping at my knee
For water from the well.

Something made me turn to the stables –
Perhaps to whisper my good morning to their
    shadows –
But mostly to crouch in the warm smell of their
    hugeness,
See the black shining of their flanks,
Their heads soft under my hand.

But nothing. Just their scent left
In the grey light scarring from the beams;
The hay yellowing the far wall, untouched,
And old Harry crying softly on an upturned stool
As somewhere a bell mourned six long times.

I did not know where they had gone then
But I cried too, somehow I understood,
Heard on the wire of the wind the sound of guns
And felt our horses, our loved lost horses
Flailing through mud, the terrible waste of mud.

◈ THE RABIES MEN

She told me how, on the coast of Ecuador,
Her father saw them in the final stages –
Their lips boiling, limbs masted to their beds
Till the last coil, the snap of the spine
Like dry wood for a fire, and that blessed end in
    death.
They were poor, these people, dark-tanned men
Who had come for a swivelful of gold from the rivers
To rich their children's lives, but they had fallen
Through empty streams to the stench of shanty
    towns,
Snatched meals over open fires, and the dogs.
The dogs were everywhere, stray things smelling
    meat,
A bubble of foam on their pink jaws snarling.
Bites took three days to bleed sanity away,
Then there was nothing but the sweet dream of Eden
That might have healed. These men's graves were
    never marked;
The dry rivers of their hands, the thirsty mouths
Swallowed by dust.

THE STRANGEST GIFT

Sister Mary Teresa gave me a wasps' nest from the
    convent garden –
Just the startings, the first leaves, a cocoon of
    whisperings –
Made out of thousands of buzzings.
To think that these yellow-black thugs
Could make such finery, such parchment,
A whole home telling the story of their days,
Written and wrought so perfect
Stung me, remembering how I'd thumped them
With thick books, reduced them to squashes on
    walls,
Nothing more than broken bits on carpets.
This little bowl, this bit of beginning
Rooted out by the gardener, reminds me
Of something bigger I keep choosing to forget,
About what beauty is, and where that beauty's found.

GEESE

This morning I caught them
Against the headlands of rain
Glowering in from the west;
Half a hundred twinklings
In the angry sky, a gust of somethings
Grey against the greyness.

And then they turned in one gust
To climb the April sky
North, becoming a sprinkling of snowflakes
Underlit, to rise into a single skein –
An arrowhead ploughing the wind.

And I knew them as geese and stood watching
Their homing for Iceland;
I stood in the first splinters of rain
Watching until they were gone
And with them all my winter.

Rumbling Bridge

One summer afternoon you go
Up the silvering of the river, low
Under the green cathedral of the leaves
Lemoned by sunlight, the slow wheel of gold
High in the huge sky.
Up there, above the flutes of the falls
You lower yourself into the delicious gasp of river
Rock downwards through stone gullies,
Fleeces of water, deep runnels, curls and eddies,
Smoothings the colour of whisky.
You stay water-tobogganing the whole day long until
    the sun
Has bled to death behind the hills,
Till the wind whispers in the trees, shudders them,
And everything is only different shades of blue.
You trail home with sandshoes
As a slip of moon lifts over the pine trees
And the bats weave their own mime through June
    air.
You come home and stand
And don't want to go inside,
Don't want to close your door on this day
Till the last of the light is lost.

THE BAT

It smelled of muslin, dank and dark,
This fallen newborn lying in the crystals
Of an early morning dew.

The size of my child's thumb;
Wings in segments that folded in on one another,
Tight beads of eyes.

In it were all the myths and legends
That had flown into the six years
Of my lying awake in the night.

But when I held it I was not afraid;
It was made of such soft intricacy
That I smoothed the fur of its head,

Whispered a prayer
As I slipped it into a grave
No larger than a snowdrop.

Capenoch Mains

Up the bumping of an ancient track
In the middle of woods and hills
A place that lay beyond time.

A house with secret doors and back stairs
With lost keys and hollow floors
Out of every book I had dreamed.

In the yard I was sure that Wallace and Bruce
Would gallop back from history;
Sweep me into the saddle and battle.

All autumn I ran the galed lanes
As winds billowed the trees and the last conkers
Thudded the mud at my feet.

At night I creaked up to the attic,
Afraid and thrilled under the breath of stars,
As an owl shuddered the dark.

December came in thick softness
Out of a hush-grey sky,
Buried us three feet deep.

Christmas was jagged glass fragments of holly,
Fires dragoning chimneys,
Carols and red candles.

◈ BEES

In winter, when the days sting white with cold,
And all the hills are glazed,
We forget them.

Then one day, without a warning,
As if the earth has tilted into light,
The birds awaken and the land is gold.

Till out of nowhere the bees hum tawny,
Drizzle through the flowers, motorway the air,
Rumble through the insides of our windows.

They are like the drones of bagpipes,
Furry things that carry in their wings
A thousand flights of pollen.

Strange that all their lives
Should be homogenised, a weight of journeys
Made sweet and pure as honey.

KILMELFORD

A bit of country soft with rain
Smelling green, ringing like glass
With the songs of warblers and wrens.

Through thigh-deep wheat fields
Columba's chapels lie still in prayer,
Fallen in on themselves with age.

Now at nightfall the boats sleep
With the white glows of their lamps
Leaning out over August lochs.

The stars flow into the water of the skies
Like pearls from a broken necklace
And the light is long, the night is huge.

THE LONG SILENCE

On Iona the last Gaelic speaker has died.
   This winter when the gales battled each roof and
   window
He was blown out and into the wind.

Once upon a time he was a tall man,
Leaning at the porch of his weaver's cottage,
His eyes like pools of the sea.

Now in the summer when the tourists come
You will hear the languages fast and loud –
But never a word of Gaelic there.

All over the western islands, they are vanishing
Like candles tonight, falling across the wind,
Their last words lost and drowned in time.

But everyone is talking, busy talking,
The radios and televisions are loud all night –
And no-one is listening to the long silence.

TORTOISESHELL

Out of the blue
On the edge of a gust of sunlight
A thing no bigger than a leaf.

It opened like a book
The brown covers of its wings
And inside I saw

The embroidered golds and oranges and blues
Of an emperor's fabled chambers –
Each lattice window finished, painted perfect.

To think this thing
No stronger than a breath,
No bigger than a single tear of paper

Had slept all winter
Hidden in some edge of dark
For this brief flurry of days

(Such little time
To learn to fly,
To dance the skies)

Only to be blown away
Like a leaf
With the first whiff of autumn.

MAY

We were coming home
On a day that swung between sun and thunder.
Sometimes the road awoke and glistened,
The song of blackbirds in the open windows
Like wet splashes, warm and soft.
And as we drove those last hills
Something in my mother broke,
Opened like a wound.
She stopped the car, her face all glassy,
In the huge banging of the wind.

Against that whole May sky she cried
So small against the hills;
Because my father was not there,
Because they could not see, together,
That place where they watched the stonechats,
The whole year greening into summer –
Larches, birches and the lambs with catkin tails.
I sat hunched in the car, hearing the huge waves
That tore from her, for all the years they loved, and
    wondered –
Do we grow wise in grief,
And where do all its rivers go?

WINTER LIGHT

to come through a low blue door
under the high grey wall of a forgotten garden
into a place in winter, roofed by grey sky
the scattered holly berries of a robin's song

nothing is alive yet, all is deep and dark
wintered and fastened, shut into the earth
a book unopened, the whole story of the year
asleep, unwritten, underneath my feet

a door in the low sky opens, sunlight
struggles to silver the ground and fades;
soft things of rain whisper and nod and sing
this is enough, this is all I ask

COLIN

He sits, waiting for his own death,
In the stubborn chair that has been his
For forty years. Ask him what happened
In June of 1932 and he will tell you
With words sharp as bullets, hard as lead –
His grey eyes will fierce you with their power.
It's the older years that just desert him now –
All his yesterdays rise up like geese across the Solway
Dissolve against the Irish Sea.
The doctor cannot heal himself (has forgotten how),
When names and dates and faces flow away
And someone else's writing reminds him who will
   call,
Who will bring his meal, what time to go to bed.
Once upon a time he strode the long, blue beaches
That now lie useless in his windows;
All he can hear are curlews
Calling his name as the dark uncurls its blanket
And the stars come out like grains of salt
In the sore wounds of the sunset.

CARSAIG

Over the edge of the moon of Mull
The talons of cliff sink into the sea.

Down below beneath the eagles
This is almost a strange Pacific.

Dripping red flowers, birdsong, ferns
In a jewellery of falls and pools.

Bees weaving their own song
In a golden cage of sunlight.

This Eden sleeping strange and rich
In the grey wolf of the Atlantic.

◈ LISTENING

That evening, the seaplane nodded on a hidden edge
    of river.
First, the two boys clambered in the back,
Scrapping like young bears.
We followed, folded in behind the dials, knees in our
    chests.
Lars steered out, hammered the plane across the
    water,
Till suddenly we rose, and all of Finnmark fell away,
The sun climbed diamond from a ledge of sky
To light a hundred lakes. Reindeer battled out
    beneath,
Streaming from the aircraft's sudden coming;
Our shadow passed across the hills –
A slow midge drifting south.

We came down on the tundra –
A white curve against the wind –
A thousand feet up, forty miles from any road.
All around the cabin nets and paddles, drums of oil,
    old wood,
Then nothing, only lake and moor and lake.

I listened, waiting for the silence, and heard instead,
A sky full of voices –
Great northern divers, phalaropes, curlews, grebes –
An ancient chorus sung
Since the beginning.

Angus McPhee of South Uist

He came from the island
Where there is bread and salt
And a huge sky blowing.
His learning was woven from those things
To wisdom, his own books.

But in the war they sent him to
Something unwound, he lost touch
With what mattered and made sense
To the schoolteacher and the priest
And the men who ploughed the seasons.

He unwound and his big blue eyes
Laughed at the spring light; they saw no longer
All that needed fetching and carrying,
That must build the drystone wall
Of their life against the wind.

So they sent him to the mainland –
The dry land –
A place of white walls and no doors,
Where he was told when he could wash his hands
Or eat his bread or sleep.

And in the dry land were other people
Who rocked backwards and forwards,
Who never stopped talking about nothing,
Whose hands had to be held
For their fear of what was not there.

And his words dried inside him
Like the flowers that blow free
On the island that brought him up.
The words stopped like water in winter
And they all poured into his hands.

In the garden he picked grasses;
He searched for tall grasses with stems,
To weave into the things he was feeling.
He made garments from grass soft as felt
Out of the pictures that grew in his hands.

But no-one could understand his language,
No-one could read his writing,
No-one tried to translate
The wild song he still wove
From the island alive inside him.

◈ SEA URCHINS

At the luminous edges of the Hebrides
Where silk water harps the shore
And the beaches are huge boomerangs
Necklaced with seaweed – they appear sometimes,
    curved things
Sharp as hedgehogs, their plates rose
And gold, or even the same green
As Venus at first light. Often
Crusts of waves crack them to pieces
Leave them in jewelled brooches
Up high beside grass and larks.
But each boy dreams of the morning
He looks down on the beach and catches
There at the lips of the water
One unbroken ball rolled
Out of the hand of the sea.

◈ VOICES

The woodpecker taps out Morse,
Crows scrawl arguing across dawn in German.

Woodpigeons make soft French love words
As little twigs of sparrows chatter in Italian.

The raven is Norse, his voice chipped from sharp
   cliffs,
And geese squabble over Icelandic sagas.

In the middle of winter all I can hear are the
   curlews,
Crying at night their Gaelic laments.

THE POTATO PICKERS

Hollows of mist; September smells so thick
Of chestnuts scudded down and leaves in wet
And water drumming choked towards the town.

Farms lie here, dark as blackened books
And dykes rib over chests of curving land
Into the rain.

Like fish creels crates are steepled
There by the field's edge. Slumped with mud
The tractor's rumbled track reflects the sky.

Now the pickers splay down in the ruts
Thudding their baskets with pale lumps
All out of shape and smooth as fossil shells.

They move like ragged crows across the day
Legs planted wide, heads slanted over rain
Until in bleary stars lights home the dusk.

DUNKELD

I cycled over the bridge,
Felt the moths furring my face.

The air was woollen with them,
That warm maroon night,

The river silvering underneath
(Midsummer and the water thin)

And up above, the swifts in sheer clouds,
Feasting on sky and moths, their dark darting

Twinkling upwards once more,
The thin shrieks of their trapezing –

Little things that have in their wings
A whole flight to Africa.

And I stood by the bridge, breathless,
Watching the river and the swifts,

My bicycle unwhirring where it leaned,
A soft bell somewhere striking midnight.

⊞ LAMB

I found a lamb
Tugged by the guyropes of the wind
Trying so hard to get up.

It was no more than a trembling bundle
A bag of bones and wet wool
A voice made of crying, like a child's.

What a beginning, what a fall,
To be born on the edge of the world
Between the sea and America.

Lamb, out of this island of stone
Yellow is coming, golden promises,
The buttery sunlight of spring.

◈ ISLAND

I remember what it was like to barefoot that house,
Wood rooms bleached by light. Days were new
    voyages, journeys,
Coming home a pouring out of stories and of
    starfish.
The sun never died completely in the night,
The skies just turned luminous, the wind
Tugged at the strings in the grass like a hand
In a harp. I did not sleep, too glad to listen by a
    window
To the sorrow sounds of the birds
As they swept down in skeins, and rose again,
    celebrating
All that was summer. I did not sleep, the weight of
    school
Behind and before too great to waste a grain of this.
One four in the morning at first larksong I went west
    over the dunes,
Broke down running onto three miles of white shell
    sand, and stood.
A wave curled and silked the shore in a single
    seamless breath.
I went naked into the water, ran deep into a green
Through which I was translucent. I rejoiced
In something I could not name; I celebrated a
    wonder
Too huge to hold. I trailed home, slow and golden,
Dried by the sunlight.

◈ WILD GOOSE CHASE

Under a bridge
Something like a print.

A paw, perhaps, passed by
At midnight, padding

North, and leaving
Just a hint of fish.

Trail all day
Catch glimpses, ripples

That could be
Might be

A piece of otter
Playing Houdini

Melted into water
Gone to ground.

◈ PENWITH

Nothing in the world could prepare you for a
    January like this –
Penzance huddled in a corner, its flags at half-mast.
The yachts in the harbour clinking and rocking
In the huge grey beast of the wind.

But inland, something else is here beside
The broken walls of the tin mines, the inked miles of
    strangeness
That wade into moorland on the edge of the sky
That has no trees, that has no heart.

The colourlessness of the land shudders –
The sun has been washed into the sea. The only light
Lies in the lions that roar and roar
Over the huge gold of Porthcurno's sands.

Except at Crean, for a moment, when something
    lifted and I looked –
A fistful of goldfinches burst like flowers
From the magic of the air and promised
Resurrection, a second chance.

THE SOMEWHERE ROAD

The car hummed out the dirt track west
And the sun was low, a ball of orange-pink
Flickering the trees and fields,
Peaching soft the level land, painting the sudden
    somewhere of a house,
Stranded in a field, deep in a sea of grass.

And every house was still a story, and in the undug
    fields
Were books, whole tomes, untouched, unwritten –
Yet I could see their edges, in stray geese and
    bobtailed deer,
And in the eyes of those who stopped beside the road
To smile, their faces made of light.

▣ IN LATE OCTOBER

On days just like this
My mother would take me at last;

A back road with bad bends,
Potholes and blind summits.

Sometimes the sun came
Like the whole of July and August,

So bright the fields and trees
Were a fierce painting of colour,

Before a thunderhead of sudden cloud
Would glower the whole valley

So the hills went into hiding
As though guilty of doing wrong.

A wind cartwheeled and roared,
Rocking the car and the woods,

Crows went wild in the sky,
Chasing for the sake of chasing.

And then at last the tree,
A crown of orange-gold light.

I scrambled out and had to slide
Under the lowest wire of a fence,

Down into a dark world, where everything
Was earthy and late October,

That bed of red-brown leaves
Hushing beneath my feet.

And there, and there, and there
Lacquered by long sleep

Mahogany conkers waiting –
Polished perfectly smooth.

I rolled them into my bag,
Loved their woody, soft knocking –

Fled back to the car
As rain splintered the windscreen;

And then as now I don't know – was it them
Or the going out there to find them?

BARVAS

A landscape battered flat by the wind;
Thistles wave their swords like Viking warriors,
Flowers hide under banks, their heads bowed.
Houses lie tousled along the roadside,
The skeletons of dead tractors and of vans
Stretching along the sparse, blown grass.
A long way west the sea combs in
Coral white, breaking on the rocks' teeth,
And the water is wolf-grey, not blue,
But pitiless, flint, the fist of the Atlantic.

◈ THE MIRACLE

It was over. They left Jerusalem in the dead of night;
no light alive, the grey rock of the last days
raw and jagged in their throats.
They were fishermen, went back, broken
to the only thing they knew, to Galilee.

And all night nothing;
the skies aubergine, a piling of bruised clouds,
the lake eerie and moonless, creeping with shadows,
the cold leaking into feet and hands like leprosy.

Dawn was a wound in the east, a gash,
the twist of a rusted knife.
And there a figure on the shore beside a fire,
someone who seemed to wait for them.
They drudged up the boats, deep into dry sand.
He spoke to them with his eyes,
gave them pieces of smoky fish.

They knew him when he called them by their names.

▣ AWAKENING

Out of twelve acorns I picked in the wood
Just one grew tall. I'd been away
The first half of July, came back
To thunder, floods, a garden gone to seed.
And then, that evening, I saw the stem
Rising high as my hand.

I bent to behold a miracle, the bitterness
Of weeds and grass all gone.
I touched three leaves – crinkled things
With cut-out edges, like those of grown-up oaks.
Eleven acorns still lay fast asleep
Deep in dark earth. One had become a tree.

THE DEATH OF COLUMBA

It was another day. The bell echoed,
A coracle came with news of Ireland
And a fine cut of meat. The sea
Wrapped round the island like a mantle of silk.

Everything he did as always, just a beat slower.
They saw nothing; the talk was generous,
The laughter easy, as a lark spun songs
Somewhere out of sky that still morning.

Yet the horse came. In the middle of it all,
And the faces turned like full moons
As that long head rested on his shoulder
And the nostrils, full of hay, flared.

For the horse had heard
Dark in the drumbeat of his heart
That edge of death, and wept
Softly against the old man's head.

Salt tears like the water that had brought him once
Out of the heart of Ireland,
That would take him now
Over a last sea, into the land he had lived.

THE WELL

I found a well once
In the dark green heart of a wood

Where pigeons ruffled up into a skylight of branches
And disappeared.

The well was old, so mossed and broken
It was almost a part of the wood

Gone back to nature. Carefully, almost fearfully,
I looked down into its depths

And saw the lip of water shifting and tilting
Heard the music of dripping stones.

I stretched down, cupped a deep handful
Out of the winter darkness of its world

And drank. That water tasted of moss, of secrets,
Of ancient meetings, of laughter,

Of dark stone, of crystal –
It reached the roots of my being

Assuaged a whole summer of thirst.
I have been wandering for that water ever since.

THE BEEHIVE CELLS

What drove their feet to these scree islands
Scarcely more than whalebacks in the sea,
To build shale haystacks under one huge grey wind,
To spend their dust of years huddled in the keen
Of sleet and rain on islands gnawed to knucklebones
Of winter gale? Nothing but this flint of faith
That lit a single flickering of lamp, and the sun
That after dark burst big and orange, beautiful
Through morning, sometimes, to everything the
    heart.

⬥ ARGYLL

All down the coast
The air was full of fish and sunset.

By nine the lemon-coloured cottages
Were warm windows glowing over the bays.

Far west the light a rim of blue and white,
Jura and Mull and Scarba all carved from shining.

On the way home we stopped to listen to the dark,
To the sea coming huge over a hundred beaches.

In among the trees, in windless stillness,
The bats were flitting, weaving patterns with the air.

That night I did not want the stars to rise at all
I wanted it to be like this and nothing more

Looking west into the sunset
To the very end of the world.

◈ THE SMALL GIANT

The otter is ninety percent water
Ten percent God.

This is a mastery
We have not fathomed in a million years.

I saw one once, off the teeth of western Scotland,
Playing games with the Atlantic –

Three feet of gymnastics
Taking on an ocean.

⊠ CALLANISH

I go back through the gate of the mind
Summer being stacked to dry in the long wind
And the stones crouched on the hill.

I am tired of history as ordered as streets;
The intact exhibits, their questions answered –
I have gone back to these stones.

They are circling in my mind as still as eagles,
And in the solstice, a gold chain of eerie light
Flickers in fires on the peat that keeps history dark.

The moors of the memories;
Faces that still have their words about them like
    bracken,
And the well there green, where the first men drank.

THE HERON

The heron is a Presbyterian minister
Standing gloomy in his long grey coat
Looking at his own reflection in a Sabbath loch.

Every now and again, pronouncing fire and
    brimstone,
He snatches at an unsuspecting trout
And stands with a lump in his throat.

The congregation of midges laughs at him in Gaelic;
He only prays for them, head bent into grey rain,
As a lark sings psalms half a mile above.

THE LILY

Last year we dug the pond –
Heaved up roots, old wire and pots,
Smoothed the deep ground, lined it,
Let water flow into its hold like liquid glass.
Your family gave you the lily for Christmas;
All winter it slept in the water,
Through the fierce blue days of January,
When ice grew thick as a doorstep there
And it seemed it would be winter for eternity.
But the year flowed slowly back in time,
Melted into the first blossom of spring,
And the geese struggled the skies for Iceland.
We had forgotten all about the lily until,
One day, it opened its heart in the middle of the sun
Like a princess, and we marvelled, laughed, came
    close
In wonderment as if some baby star
Had crashed into our grass and stayed alight.
For four whole days we were like our own children
And the lily was the centre of the world.

◈ THE SEA

That day after the rain turned the river to a dash of
    gravel
We drove down to the sea,
Past the villages that lay like clamshells in the
    sunlight,
By little single tracks of sand
That wound down to the wide blue basin of the sea.

That day the sea smelled of the fields,
Of hay and loam, of inland and the rain,
Not salty but sweet –
And I believed as I smelled it
It would taste fresh and good if I drank it.

MRS JAMES

Once a week I go for logs
To the old rectory at the end of the street.

She does not need the wood, she says,
She has not used the room or lit the fire

Since 1956. When I carry up the logs
She tells me how she had to work from six to
   midnight

In the war, how the south of England suffered,
How her brother was among the first to enter
   Belsen,

How he came back like a shadow of himself
And never spoke of it again.

Now her house is fast asleep. Not
In our world; it smells still of the 1930s:

Dead petals on the windowsills, dust
Dancing in the air where sunlight

Falls in slats from the high windows.
She is caught in her own war

To remember and preserve those days
Like butterflies, like pressed flowers, like leaves.

Every time I go for logs I enter
The great stopped clock of her house,

And breathe, a little afraid, a little thrilled
The stories that are written in the air,

Then go down softly for the logs her brother stacked
Forty years ago, the day before he died.

⬙ THAT YEAR

The plough hit a hollowness,
A missing thing whose sound stopped him,
Brought him to his knees,
His both hands dragging that wet blackness back.

A hole in the earth. Seven, and the last light
Honeyed from the west across the fields.
He heard his heart; lowered himself through the
    emptiness,
Dropped into the softness of a cave kept silent
Who knew how many hundred years.

His eyes saw only darkness, then slowly woke, found
    walls
Curving the place to a beehive, a cupped heart
Woven out of careful stone, shaped smooth to
    something
Whose name was buried with the hands that built it.

Yet all at once he knew what this had been;
The whispers, soft as candle flames, breathed his
    hearing,
A peace shone from the dark and welled his heart
So full he dragged the tangle of his hat away, stood
    bowed,
As somewhere up above the curlews flew their
    evensong.

A Poem for Ann

Three feet small
With dreams as big as Christmas.

A cornfield of curls
And a smile that would melt a soldier.

When you cry
All of you falls to pieces;
Everyone comes running to mend you.

At night your eyes look huge;
You are afraid of the owl
That ghosts your bedroom window.

I tell you a story
But you are kingdoms and princes away
Long before the ending.

In the morning I will bring you blackbirds
And put the sun on your pillow.
I will tie your laces,
And pray safe roads for your feet.

TOBERMORY

August and the warm rain
Rubbed the sky like soft hair.

All around the bay
A ring of smudged blue houses;

Out in the shallows, yachts and masts
Breathing up and down and up.

At nightfall you and I circled
The whole horseshoe of the harbour

Listening to songs from upper rooms,
Gaelic, the laughter of deep red windows;

The rain, gentle as felt, touching our faces,
Webs of rain that came in fingertips –

As the dark swelled like a bruise and the bay filled
    with candles,
And we walked back, talking of nothing and
    everything

In the soft blue rain
And the rising of the moon.

⬧ THE ISLAND

We came to the island
Reluctant, dragged our feet
Up over the gravel shore.

Three nights we remained
In the monastery's rattling emptiness
Our heads shorn cold, ears echoing song.

The wind came like scurrying creatures
Gnawing at fingers and feet;
Milk-blue moonlight filled the cloisters.

We prayed, and at first our prayers
Were ragged things, torn thoughts
That blew into the fierce dark.

Then in the waking pain of the second night
Something broke the jar of my heart;
A softness flowed I had not known before.

On the third day I walked to the south end,
Met the sea leaping in fierce dogs –
My hands felt skiffed like flints.

But not only my hands.
I came back from the island, all of us came back
Glass vessels, see-through, clear.

▨ The Search

we have to go so far for silence
have to row a long way out to listen
spoon and spoon the water till we dip the oars

about, above, blue nothingness
an orange edge against the sky
the tips of slow gulls leaving light

ledges of gold light that change and flash
in this last softening of sun
a rippled mirror all the way across

this somewhere in between the night and day;
then row slow home, and row slow home
soundless, leaving the sea unbroken.

▨ CALF

Born with everything but breath
He slid into the world a month too soon.

The trees traced with snow, the farm white-roofed,
Even the tractor buried useless.

The far mountains gullied white,
Lost under an avalanche of cloud.

And the calf nothing more than a flow of soft water,
Eyes thin against the light.

Carried like a slack brown sack
Out over the crackling field.

AGNES

That summer in St Andrews
As the sea was combing in white furls
The beach, and the wind was combing
Wild and white your hair's last curls,
I pushed you in your wheeled chair
Not knowing what to talk about,
Knowing only I would not see you there again.

And you tried to remember;
You tried to pull together, like blankets and old
     shawls,
Names and memories and years.
And all of them just blew away like gulls
Across the sea, and when you smiled
It was a child that smiled at me.

◈ SOMETIMES

In
all
the
rush
and
hurry
of
our
lives
we
need
so
much
just
now
and
then
to
find
an

island

◈ SEPTEMBER

The fields lay white beneath a snow of sun
And birds were restless underneath, they rose and
    wheeled
Like silver leaves. The skies were more than blue;
Burnished and beaten with a strange brilliance.
The angels are coming, I thought;
The angels will come in the night
When a huge moon ovals through these bright and
    cloudless skies;
They will come to bind the sheaves
While we are fast asleep.
They will work the fields, their wings tight-folded,
All through the white night of this September,
The moon gliding high like a balloon
Over the glazed harvest of the world;
Nothing moving except the angels and the wind,
    until the task is done
In the warm stillness of the dawn.

◈ A Poem for Ivars

A picture of Latvia:
You as a boy lifting potatoes behind a horse,
Swallows ticking wings in a farmyard sky,
The generals of winter a day yet closer.

In the hungry faces, the simple hands,
And this hard road through the furrows of Moscow,
I see richer earth still living, wooden songs
That could pull your people's faith.

If a man should come now to your door
Selling motorways, a rustle of money in his eyes;
Do not buy his road, for it leads
To all our lost riches, our need of God.

GAELIC

It lies in pockets in the hills,
A wink of gold that has not been panned
From the older veins and worn faces.

And sometimes on a dark river of night
I imagine it returning from the seas in its struggle
Like salmon to the birthright of the springs.

THE COLOURISTS

They came out here in the first years of the century,
Their eyes still drunk on Paris and Venice –
Here to the edge of the world, this blowing place,
Where the days are a constant gale,
Where everything is always changing
In a flurry of bright gusts.

They came out here
To put easels into the north wind and try to catch it,
To haul colours from sky and sea,
Tie them down to canvases – shreds of them,
Tattered edges – and take them back
In something that lasted forever.

THE STRANGER

All winter he braved the barn, took
The scuffings from our breadboard, the pecks
Meant for sparrows.
He'd come to work with wood, he said,
And brought us a table smelling still of cherry
From a tree blown down in mid-November storm.
The lambs nibbled the air about him, curious,
Let him touch their thin, milky bleats
With the big softness of his hands.
We eyed him, hovering,
Through the slats of the wood, awed
And wondering. When he made mud doves,
Cupped them in his hand and let them fly –
Laughed like a whole field of sunlight.

◈ TRUST

Five days the snow had lain
Deep as a boot. Mouths of ice
Hung from roofs and windows,
The river slid by like a wolf.

At noon I went out with crumbs
Cupped in one hand. As I crouched,
A robin fluttered from nowhere,
Grasped the landfall of my palm.

A rowan eye inspected me
Side on. The blood-red throat
Swelled and sank, breathing quickly,
Till hungry, the beak stabbed fast.

The robin finished, turned,
Let out one jewel of sound,
Then ruffled up into the sky –
A skate on the frosty air.

◈ SEEING

The first time I saw them I was only three.
My father curled me out of bed,
Hoisted me on rounded shoulders
Up to the silver dark of the attic.
I was still nine-tenths asleep, in a far away
That furred my words and thoughts.

The dusty shadows of boxes and carpets and trains.
I heard the house gurgle and hiss;
Smelled the apples, moist and soft in their wrapped
    silence.

He held me high to the angled window,
Up into the fork of the roof.
I looked, searching,
For what he might want me to find.

Only the stars crackled and sparked
Above the grey shapes of the gardens.
The wind shifted restless in the trees.

Then something else, things
Swimming, hunching from the north,
Their underwings sheened in moonlight,
Beating that midnight in waves – fifty, a hundred,
    more –
Deep through the water of our sky, passing at last
Into someone else's night.

I followed them with my finger,
Knowing this was why I was there;
My father down below, beseeching me –
Did you see them? Did you see the geese?

⬧ Eleventh November

That November morning
It had not dawned, dark
Was heavy on the trees
Velveting the road.

The car furred into the distance,
Lights opening in wool whiteness
Corners, bringing flickers of tree and hill
Out of them, moments of sharpness.

Like that I caught the fox
Curled in prayer;
Gloved by the shadows,
The blink of a picture –

The red beneath his head
Where the car had banged
To break his run, his breath–
Leave him on the hard shoulder,

A question, cold and still.
But all that dawn, that day,
Was changed – echoed, remembered –
The world was a fox smaller.

◈ TRAVELLERS

When the women came to the door
You could always tell who they were.
Something in the hair, the eyes,
That hadn't settled, that was not mortgaged
To a town. They carried baskets,
Clothes, toys – poor things for a few pence.

My mother asked them in,
Gave them broth on wild, November days
That blustered wind and rain about the house.
She never sent them off without some gift;
They thanked her with their smoky voices, rough,
And as I watched them I thought they looked like
    horses,
Unbroken horses that didn't fear the fields,
That could sleep easy in the lee of hills,
Ride from stable to stable,
Rough-shod.

Their men met them on the corners,
Red with drink. They disappeared, all of them
    together,
Like autumn leaves.

THE JOURNEY

That is not what I remember:
For me the dark watchfulness of strangers,
The tiredness of towns
Full of their own emptiness,
The desire to keep our journey secret as our gifts.

The morning we arrived
I smelled oranges in the fields,
The sun rose through the mist in a disc of gold,
Our feet scuffed the stubbled fields
And a blind man sang all alone
In the middle of the nowhere of the streets.

They were asleep too when we came,
One dusty beam of sun lancing the floor;
They were a painting already, their story
Frozen in the stone of legend –
Stranger than itself, yet made
Of nothing but its own simplicity.

We had thought God above all this
And we were wrong. We went home
Confused, following no star, wondering
Where we were going. I lay at night
Seeing the eyeless socket of the moon,
Watching the vast emptiness of the dark,
Unblinking. It was in the beggars,

The sore emptiness of hunger in the homes we
    passed,
I saw my blindness.

That was the beginning of the journey.

LUSKENTYRE

On a day the wind comes from everywhere
And the sea is a rugged fleece,
The bell flows over the island
And the black suits and the black hats go
Slow to the church at the top of the beach.

The psalms lift and fall in long waves,
And after the minister's words are blown away
In the field of stones like broken teeth,
They go back to the warmth of the hall.

The tea is poured like liquid peat into white cups,
And there is talk, the soft water of Gaelic,
As through the advent calendar window
The hill is sugared with snow
And flakes chase the air like birds.

JURA

From Carsaig you can see it,
Three peaks rising up out of the Atlantic,
Like a sea monster, the ridge of a dragon's back.
What is there to find but a scattering of houses,
A road, a hotel, then nothing.
It drifts into mist, a huge loneliness,
Composed of bracken and moor and cave.
Who comes to look? Who bothers
To cross the few sea miles
To watch some great mound of empty stone
Drift into the distance?
This busy world would think it worthless –
A barren landfall on the edge of sanity.
To me it is wondrous that such things should still
    remain,
Uncharted and untamed, like eagles.

◈ PEARLS

They were the reason the Romans came here –
River things, spun into milky globes over years and
    years.
I often wonder who it was who found them first,
Those mussels, dark shells whorled and folded
Like hands in prayer, embedded in feet of shingle.

The travellers knew where they were. The unsettled
    people
Who followed the seasons, the stars, yearned only
    the open road.
They carried the knowledge of pearls inside them,
    secret,
Could tell the very bend of river each pearl had come
    from –
This one like the pale globe of Venus at dawn,
This one a skylark's egg, and this the blush of a
    young girl's lips.

Yet the Romans never reached the Highland rivers
Where the best pearls slept. They were kept out
By the painted people, the Pictish hordes
Bristling on the border like bad weather.

The pearls outlived even the travellers, whose
    freedom
Was bricked into the big towns long enough ago,
Who did not understand any longer
The language of the land.

In the last part of the north,
In the startling blue of the rivers
The shells still grow. Their pearls are stories
That take a hundred years to tell.

THE MUSIC

He got his tunes that way;
He heard them,
As though they were edges of wind,
As if he saw the notes
In the loud rattle of the storm,
In the darkness – coming out of nothing.
He listened for them, as though they were bees
In ones and twos to begin with,
Then a swarm, a black net, a mist.
He had to catch them in the bow of his fiddle,
He had to find them before they passed,
Were gone and lost forever.

Where did they come from, those notes?
It was as though they had been sent to find him
Through the rampaging of Atlantic gales,
Or else had blown off course
Like a ship's cargo, like a pirate treasure hold,
Had spilled onto St Kilda, into his hands,
Into the fiddle,
Till it was filled brimful.

He wrote none of them down.
He caught them when they came;
He caught them in the net of his listening,
Recognised and remembered them,
Stored them in his head as the others
Stored fish and birds for winter.

They lay in the dark of his head
Like gold in the depths of a cave.
They died with him too
The day his eyes glazed and their light
Failed and faded for ever. The tunes were blown out
And back into the wind.

IONA

Is this place really nearer to God?
Is the wall thin between our whispers
And his listening? I only know
The world grows less and less –
Here what matters is conquering the wind,
Coming home dryshod, getting the fire lit.
I am not sure whether there is no time here
Or more time, whether the light is stronger
Or just easier to see. That is why
I keep returning, thirsty, to this place
That is older than my understanding,
Younger than my broken spirit.

◼ HEBRIDES

This shattered place, this place of fragments,
A play of wind and sea and light,
Shifting always, becoming and diminishing;
Out of nowhere the full brightness of morning
Blown away, buried and lost.

And yet, if you have faith, if you wait long enough,
There will be the miracle of an otter
Turning water into somersaults;
The jet blackness of a loch brought back to life
By the sudden touch of sun.

But you will take nothing home with you
Save your own changedness,
And this wind that will waken you
Sometimes, all your life, yearning to return.

THE PICTS

They do not speak to us
But stare down the centuries, dark as stone;

Leave only hints and flickers of themselves
In riddles of painted birds and battles,

Little whispers
Embedded in the placenames of the east.

If one day we make a machine
That unpicks the sounds asleep in wood and stone

We'll dig for words in the ochre fields they left –
Fragments, thin as flints –

Half-heard and muffled words
To be gathered in baskets, brought back

And rebuilt like a broch, to interlock
So we can re-enter the world of their time

And listen to them at last.

❖ REMEMBER

There will be only a few days like this –
The low sun flinting the house
Through the green sea of the trees as you stand
Struck, blessed, bathed in the same light
That rose life once from the young earth, that appled
The first child's cheeks.
There will be only a few days like this
To stop doing and stand, blinking,
As the leverets tumble in the bright field
And a cuckoo's moss voice calls from a far wood.
Wait until the sun has gone in broken orange
Down beneath the hills, and the blue sky
Hurts with the sudden shudder of the dusk.
Give thanks and turn and go back home –
For there will be only a few days like this.

▨ PRAYER

If you do not believe in God
Go on a blue spring day across these fields:
Listen to the orchids, race the sea, scent the wind.

Come back and tell me it was all an accident
A collision of blind chance
In the empty hugeness of space.

The Novemberland

Something wonderful there is in coming home
A ragged, late November night,

Leaving town and entering a midnight black,
Rain splintering the glass.

Headlights dig from darkness two white beams,
Rendering the other outer world so huge,

The car panthering the lanes,
Tunnelling a dusk that's roofed with branches.

Furry paws of wind come and nudge the car,
The trees above all wave like soundless cries.

And then an owl, a padded softness of a thing,
Suddens the eyes, glides through light and vanishes.

Until a long hour afterwards, at last,
Home's amber cave floods whole the heart,

Tyres crackle gravel and the engine shudders still,
A crystalling of stars engulfs the sky –

And silence pours back in to fill the night.

⊠ THIS YEAR

not before January the snow
a day thin blue as a bird's shell

the skies grazed with storm
a great grey closing over the sea

not more than flickers of skin
thin on the wind

then flocking the air, lashes of cotton
pattering and soft

settling over us, a blanket of silence
filling the trees with shapes

when night cleared in a clustering of stars
the roads deep and the power gone

I realised we had not come far at all

BELIEVING

Winter and the geese circle the fields in hunching
   skeins,
Everything asleep and buried, secret,
Waiting for some silent voice to waken them once
   more.

There among the trees, low above the ground,
The sun struggles to break through,
Pale as a daffodil, frail and failing.

To keep believing is not easy, even in December
With the child's clutter of star and donkey, gift and
   manger.
The dark comes back, the long dark

Searching lost through the fields. The night
Starless and empty, just rivers full of gibberish,
The morning hopeless, a grey sky low over a grey
   earth.

So was it just a story written long ago
Lost in the telling? Yet why then did they carry it
With such fire, dying to lions and the torment

Of wheels and spikes? Why if all of it
Was nothing more than stories?
Will not Christ return?

Two thousand years have come and gone
Yet will it happen on some late November night,
A light among the trees when all the fields are
    flooded;

Something to go and seek and find
Alone, that happens just to those
Who leave everything they have behind?

◈ REMEMBERING THE AMISH

And I have seen them coming home on summer
    nights
Or bent above the washbowl in the kitchen,
Haloed in the window by the low sun's leaving;
Soft voices in the fields of gentle men with horses.

And in the town they walk their own way,
As though a reverence for what lies beneath their
    feet
Is in their shoes, and in their eyes a peace
No man may buy and few have ever found.

And sometimes when I meet them I feel like him
    who went
With all his father's wealth and lived in laughter far
    away
And woke one day to find he'd nothing left.
I feel like turning just like him for home –

That I may also start again.

◈ SNATCHES OF SONG

Eight goldfinches,
Strung out along the telegraph wires
One October morning of gale:
Notes in the storm's tune.

Also by KENNETH STEVEN

Iona

9780715207789

This bestselling collection of poems draws on Kenneth's long association with the west coast of Scotland and with Iona in particular, a place that has been of deep spiritual significance and inspiration since his early childhood.

'An excellent collection ... Steven has a talent for capturing the startling, original image, like a sudden revelation, and placing it in beautifully observed pictures of the world around us. He is a fine, fine poet and this new volume is highly recommended.'

The New Shetlander

Iona – CD

9780715208847

Kenneth's beautiful poetry comes to life in this captivating recording of some of his best-loved poems, influenced by the west of Scotland and by Iona in particular.

www.standrewpress.com

Also by KENNETH STEVEN

Columba

Poems

9780715208229

Kenneth takes us on Columba's journey to the west coast of Scotland. He takes us on a plethora of other journeys too – both real and imagined, ancient and modern. Images of secret places from the west coast, from its Celtic legacy, and from the lives of the people still there today, are all powerfully evoked in this collection.

Wild Horses

Illustrations by John Busby

9780715207987

This volume contains the best-loved of Kenneth's wildlife and landscape poems. The collection is suffused with a gentle spirituality and celebrates the seasons of Highland Scotland that he loves.

The collection is beautifully illustrated by internationally renowned wildlife artist John Busby, in a unique collaboration of poetry and art.

Salt and Light

9780715208427

The Celtic Christian world and the islands of the Hebrides inspired many of these beautiful, evocative poems. Some recreate those early Celtic days in Ireland and in western Scotland, others are concerned with the finding of God's presence in our lives amidst the ordinary and the everyday. All are about moments of transformation and the finding of faith amid our human struggle.

www.standrewpress.com

Greetings Cards

Six designs, each featuring a beautiful poem by Kenneth Steven

Iona
KENNETH STEVEN
6-pack folded cards with envelopes
Featuring the poem 'Iona'
Blank for your own message
9780715209196
£6.99

Voices
KENNETH STEVEN
6-pack folded cards with envelopes
Featuring the poem 'Voices'
Blank for your own message
9780715209165
£6.99

Islands
KENNETH STEVEN
6-pack folded cards with envelopes
Featuring the poem 'Islands'
Blank for your own message
9780715209219
£6.99

Hebrides
KENNETH STEVEN
6-pack folded cards with envelopes
Featuring the poem 'Hebrides'
Blank for your own message
9780715209202
£6.99

The Small Giant
KENNETH STEVEN
6-pack folded cards with envelopes
Featuring the poem 'The Small Giant'
Blank for your own message
9780715209189
£6.99

Daffodils
KENNETH STEVEN
6-pack folded cards with envelopes
Featuring the poem 'Daffodils'
Blank for your own message
9780715209172
£6.99

Assorted Cards
KENNETH STEVEN
6-pack assorted folded cards with envelopes
Blank for your own message
9780715209288
£6.99

Sanctuary – CD

Poems of Celtic Spirituality

9780715208410

Kenneth reads 20 of his favourite poems, accompanied by music and by the sounds of sea and land. He also gives a sense of the stories behind the poems, and a background to his own life and inspiration.

Making the Known World New

Poetry and prose

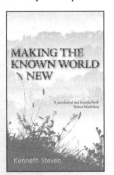

9780715208823

When he moved house, Kenneth Steven left behind him the small square of ground that had been his garden for many years: a place of solitude, contemplation, observance and simple relaxation – a place for the mind to wander as the seasons pass.

In *Making the Known World New*, this small oasis inspires reflections full of wonder at the variety, determination and sheer audacity of nature in a confined space. The garden kindles thoughts of the wider world and the threat it faces.

www.standrewpress.com